Say Hello to Baby

For Smitha and Swapna –
the BEST big sisters
in the world – S.P-H. xx

For Jodie, Wilf and Rafe – B.T.

First published in Great Britain in 2020 by Wren & Rook

Text copyright © Smriti Prasadam-Halls, 2020
Illustration copyright © Britta Teckentrup, 2020

The right of Smriti Prasadam-Halls and Britta Teckentrup to be identified as
author and illustrator respectively of this work has been asserted by them in
accordance with the Copyright, Designs and Patents Act 1988.

HB ISBN: 978 1 5263 6194 3
PB ISBN: 978 1 5263 6195 0
E-book ISBN: 978 1 5263 6193 6
10 9 8 7 6 5 4 3 2 1

MIX
Paper from
responsible sources
FSC® C104740
FSC
www.fsc.org

Wren & Rook
An imprint of
Hachette Children's Group
Part of Hodder & Stoughton
Carmelite House
50 Victoria Embankment
London EC4Y 0DZ

An Hachette UK Company
www.hachette.co.uk
www.hachettechildrens.co.uk

Publishing Director: Debbie Foy
Editors: Liza Miller and Phoebe Jascourt
Art Director: Laura Hambleton
Designer: Sally Griffin

Printed in China

smriti prasadam-halls • britta teckentrup

Say Hello to Baby

wren & rook

Congratulations!

You're a **big brother** or **sister**.

Life will never be the same again – it's going to be even **better** than before!

Watching someone grow up is **amazing**. You will see your little brother or sister change a lot over time, and you'll get to know each other better and better each day.

It's going to be a journey filled with **fun**. Are you ready to begin?

Give Baby a gentle hug and kiss to say hello.

Having a baby at home might feel **exciting**...

... but it might also feel **strange**. That's okay! If you have questions, make sure you ask them all.

It may seem like a lot has changed, but one thing that hasn't changed at all is how much you are loved. Your parents may have their hands full but, no matter what, they are still full of **love** for you.

Babies need to do lots of **sleeping** and **feeding** at first, so you may not be able to play together right away. But don't worry, very soon they'll be ready for action!

Until then, ask a grown-up to help you choose a toy for Baby. Or why not draw a picture to welcome them home?

All babies **grow** and **change** differently.

Some babies will be on the move as soon as they can,

while others may prefer to sit still.

Some babies will make lots of noise,

while others may enjoy quietly watching and listening.

There's no need to worry if Baby isn't doing the same things as other babies you meet. Each tiny tot changes and develops when they're ready – not a moment sooner!

Your important job is to have **fun** with Baby and get ready to teach them lots of **exciting** new things.

Did you know?

A baby's **eye colour** can change over time. Some are born with blue eyes, but these may become brown or green later.

Babies are born with more **bones** than grown-ups. Over time, some of the very small bones join together and become one.

In the womb, babies are attached to their mum by a bendy tube called the **umbilical cord**. Once they are born they don't need it any more, and the place where it once sat becomes Baby's **belly button**!

Even though babies sound like they're crying from the moment they're born, they don't actually produce **tears** until a few weeks have passed.

Babies don't always like peace and quiet. Sometimes they enjoy background noises, such as the **hum** of a radio or the **whoosh** of a washing machine.

Growth and health

Babies grow quickly in their first year. Within six months, many are twice as heavy as when they were born. By the time they are a year old, they are three times as heavy.

That's like growing from the length of a **mouse** to a **cat** in just one year!

170
160
150
140
130
120
110
100
90
80
70
60

During the first few months, grown-ups will measure Baby's height and weight a lot. This is to make sure that they're healthy and strong.

Do you know how **heavy** and **tall** you are?

When they are a few weeks old, babies are given their first special injections called **immunisations**. These keep people well and protect them from illnesses.

What do you do to stay **healthy**?

Babies have tiny fingers and toes – but have you noticed how large their **head** is? It holds a very big brain to help them learn.

Put your fingers and toes next to Baby's. Are yours a lot bigger?

Thoughts and feelings

When we want to say how we feel, we use **words**. Babies don't have the words yet to say what they're thinking, but they can make **signals** with their face and voice to let us know what they need.

Baby's earliest signal is a cry. But don't worry – this doesn't always mean they're unhappy. Sometimes it means they're **hungry, tired** or that they need to have their **nappy changed**…

…and sometimes they might just be bored!

When Baby **smiles** or **giggles**, they're enjoying what they're doing. Sometimes they might also do this to copy someone else. It's their way of joining in.

Can you make Baby smile or laugh?

I spy with my little eye

When babies are first born, they can't see as many colours as you can. Their sight is blurry to begin with, so they like to look at things with big areas of **light** and **dark**.

Can you **draw** some black and white animals for Baby to look at?

Babies also enjoy watching things that **move**, such as a turning mobile or a gently swaying tree. They might even stare at your finger if you move it slowly from side to side.

Try dangling a little **toy** for Baby to watch.

Babies love looking at **patterns**, **photos** and **faces**. In fact, one of their favourite faces to look at is their own!

You could sit in front of a mirror together and make some **funny faces**.

After a few months, Baby will be able to see lots of colours and will want to look at everyone and everything. Sometimes they'll look around so much they'll get very sleepy!

Why don't you show Baby your favourite **book** and point out all the exciting pictures?

Sounds and songs

Babies can already hear well when they are born. They could even hear voices and sounds around them when they were in the womb!

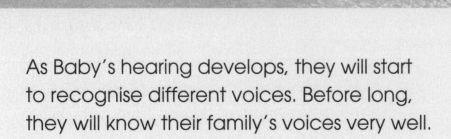

As Baby's hearing develops, they will start to recognise different voices. Before long, they will know their family's voices very well.

Little ones like listening to **stories**. Can you tell Baby a story right now?

Babies like listening to all sorts of sounds. They love music and different instruments, such as bells, rattles and the **tip-tap** rhythm of a drum.

Can you make some music for Baby? Try not to be too noisy – a very **big bang** can be scary!

One of Baby's favourite sounds is **singing**. They love listening to nursery rhymes and songs. As they get older, they may try to clap along and join in.

Let's sing Baby a **lullaby** to help them fall asleep.

Dinner time!

Milk is the only food that babies have during their first few months. It gives them all the goodness they need to grow **healthy** and **strong**. They drink milk from their mum's breast or formula milk from a bottle.

At around six months old, babies are ready to eat other things. They start with simple, soft foods such as mashed vegetables and porridge. It can get **very messy**!

Show Baby how nicely you can eat your meals. Now try and help Baby hold a spoon.

Once they have **teeth** to bite and chew with, babies can eat lots more foods. It can be painful – and dribbly – when new teeth are coming through.

Sometimes Baby will cry because their gums are sore – be **patient** with them.

Babies love to feed themselves with foods they can hold, such as strips of toast and chunks of fruit.

Choose some tasty finger foods to nibble along with Baby!

Talkative tots

Learning to **talk** is tricky, so babies start off with sounds that slowly become words.

The first sounds that babies make are **ooohs** and **aaaahs**. This is called **cooing**.

Babies make all sorts of other sounds with their lips, tongue and teeth as they learn to talk. Sometimes they even blow raspberries!

Can you blow **raspberries** with Baby?

As babies develop, they will copy the sounds they hear around them. This is called **babbling**. They might not know any proper words yet, but that doesn't stop them!

Mum

or

Dad

might be the first thing Baby says.

Listen out for Baby's first words!

Over time, they will be able to say more words. They might even invent their own names for people and things that are **special** to them.

Can you teach Baby to say **your name**?

On the move

There's no telling exactly when babies will start **moving**, but once they start, there's no stopping them. Some crawl on their hands and knees, and others push themselves along on their bottoms. They can be **very fast** – so watch out!

Try **crawling** or **pushing** along with Baby!

Soon after this, Baby may stand. They do this by grabbing tightly on to a **chair**, **table** or **person**, and pulling themselves up. They stay standing for longer each time they practise.

Clap your hands whenever Baby stands up!

After they stand, babies will soon take their **first steps**. They will probably be very wobbly and fall down quite a lot!

Hold on to Baby's hand and take a walk around the room.

Learn and play

Babies are **learning** all the time, even when it looks like they're just having fun. Kicking around on a baby mat helps little ones **exercise** and build **strength**.

Lie on your back with Baby and see the world from down there. Why not **kick** along with them?

Reaching for a book or grabbing hold of your finger helps babies to develop **hand-eye coordination**. Their brain, eyes and hands are sending and receiving important signals.

Practise **building** a tower with blocks and then see if Baby can knock it down!

As babies grow, they will get better at using their hands. This means that when they're older, they will be able to dress and feed themselves.

Find different materials for Baby to touch and explore. Try things that are **squishy, bumpy, hard** and **crinkly**.

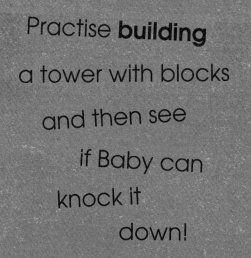

Fun and games

Babies love to **play**! Try some of these games, but don't forget to ask a grown-up first.

Singing and dancing

Sing Baby a **nursery rhyme** with actions. Baby will love watching your fingers wiggling and waving. Soon they will be joining in too!

Peekaboo

Babies love **surprises**! Hide your face behind your hands, then open them up and say 'Peekaboo!'. You can also hide a teddy behind your back, then bring it forward and say, 'Peekaboo!'.

Animal noises

Make as many **animal sounds** as you can, and see if Baby joins in. Sounds such as 'moo', 'baa' and 'woof' are fun for Baby to say. Why not find some animal pictures to go with the noises?

Ball-rolling

Once Baby is old enough to sit on the floor safely, you can play some gentle **ball games**. Roll a soft ball slowly towards Baby and see if they can roll it back to you. It may take a few tries!

Bedtime stories

Can you help tell Baby your favourite **bedtime story**? They might not understand all of the words, but they will love listening to you tell it.

After a while, you'll notice that Baby is less of a **little baby** and more of a **little person**. But they will still be learning and changing all the time – the fun doesn't stop here!

Baby will spend less time napping and more time trying to get around. They'll also be more talkative and ready to play. They'll need your **top tips** on everything from putting on their shoes to learning to count.

Help Baby along, but remember they may want to try things on their own. They won't always succeed, so be ready for tears. It can be hard not getting things right.

Here are some things you can do with Baby once they're a bit older:

Colouring in a picture – Baby may not be able to stay inside the lines, but it will be a lot of fun!

Doing a puzzle – help Baby fit the pieces.

Splashing in small puddles – make sure you're wearing your wellies!

There are lots more fun things you can do with Baby, but the most important thing to do is enjoy getting to know them.

And remember, this special someone isn't just a little brother or sister ...

... they're a best friend for ever.